los angeles
2nd edition

eat.shop los angeles was researched,
photographed and written by agnes baddoo

eat

shop

about eat.shop

the first thing to know about the *eat.shop guides* is that they are the only guides dedicated to just eating and shopping. okay, we list some hotels, because we know that you need to sleep. and don't forget to whittle out some time for cultural activities—all of the businesses featured in the book are helmed by creative types who are highly influenced by the arts and sights of the cities they live in—culture is good for you.

the *eat.shop guides* feature approximately 90 carefully picked businesses, all of them homegrown and distinctive. some are small and some are big. some are posh and some are street-style. some are spendy and some require nothing more than pocket change. some are old school and some are shiny and new. some are hip and some are under-the-radar. point being, we like to feature a mix of places that are unique because you can feel the passionate vision of the owners from the moment you step through their door, eat their food, touch their wares.

enough explaining, here are a couple of things to remember when using this guide: remember that hours change seasonally, so always call or check the website before you go. we apologize if a featured business has closed. being a small business can be a rough road and some of our featured ones don't make it—so use this book often and support the little guys! remember that items mentioned may not be available any longer, but there will most likely be something equally fantastic available. finally, each guide has a two-year life span, and each new edition is different than the last—so when the 2nd edition of eat.shop los angeles comes out in 2009, make sure to keep this first edition as it will still be useful.

agnes's notes on los angeles

sprawling would be an understatement to describe los angeles. from the first moment i visited almost twenty years ago, i knew i wanted to live in this city where the desert and the mountains meet the ocean. though i love my hometown of new york city with all its culture, diversity and immediacy; the narrowness, congestion and weather finally got to me—in this agreeable setting i can still pursue a vast array of cosmopolitan activites.

in the fourteen years i've lived here, i've seen the city transform from a small number of well-known commercial areas with vast residential neighborhoods between, to virtually every neighborhood having a pedestrian commercial center where you can walk about and explore the offerings. this development has made these neighborhoods diversity and vibrancy apparent. any excuse to get out the car and interact with people while erranding or shopping is a good thing. and yes, while still sprawling, these pedestrian clusters make l.a. seem more intimate.

i was fortunate to have great friends introduce me to l.a.'s splendors when i first arrived, as many of this citys' best haunts have little street presence. i hope this guide, which is full of my favorite spots, in my favorite areas of the city, will be that friend for you. eat. shop. enjoy!

agnes baddoo
agnes@eatshopguides.com

the master list

malibu / topanga / santa monica / brentwood

eat:

café mimosa
malibu seafood
port royal
vincenti

shop:

apartment number 9
marie mason
post26
sugar paper
turpan
zenbunni gallery

venice / mar vista / culver city

eat:

axe
baby blues bar-b-q
bluebird café
beechwood
empanada's place
ford's filling station
stroh's gourmet
3 square bakery + café / röckenwagner bakery

shop:

firefly
pamela barish
patio culture
surfas
the stronghold 1895
tortoise

fairfax district / mid-city / hollywood

eat:

beverly hills juice
bld
bob's coffee and donuts
boule
chameau
dominick's
inaka
little next door
lou
magnolia
mao's kitchen
milk
moishe's / moishe's village
the hungry cat

shop:

black sheep knittery
calleen cordero
claire joseph
des kohan
family
healing waters
hillary rush
ige
krislyn design
lost and found stores
marcjoseph/kate
momo/shabon
mrs. biederhof's
particolare
persimmon
plastica
reserve
scent bar
scout
union

los feliz/atwater village / silver lake / echo park / eagle rock

eat:

alcove cafe & bakery
auntie em's kitchen
cafe tropical
canele
colorado wine company
delilah bakery
square one dining
the cheese store of silverlake
the oinkster

shop:

a+r
bon & ging
carol young undesigned
distant
flounce vintage
gypsy's palace
keep
panty raid
paulina quintana
show
steinberg & sons / the little knittery
10 ten

west adams

shop:

plant maple skate & surf shop

boyle heights / chinatown / downtown

eat:

izayoi
la serenata de garibaldi
pacific dining car
via cafe

shop:

blend / 06+
dosa818
loft appeal
push emporium

this list shows all businesses by neighborhood.

agnes's twenty favorite things

01 > ahi burger at malibu seafood

02 > pear double ginger banana manna shake at beverly juice bar

03 > jambon buerre at little next door

04 > trout dinner special with chocolate tofu mousse dessert at inaka

05 > filet mignon, baked potato and tart tartin at pacific dining car

06 > dark and stormy at the hungry cat

07 > chocolate panna cotta with caramel sauce at dominick's

08 > guava pastries at café tropical

09 > coffee crunch ice cream with coffee macaroon sandwich at milk

10 > seared trout, braised leeks and potato at canele

11 > vivienne westwood plaid bathrobe dress at scout

12 > hazel brown shearling patchwork jacket at +06

13 > pippa small 24 karat gem ring at dosa818

14 > bed and bath textiles at distant

15 > kate double-layer silk charmeuse shirt gown at pamela barish

16 > madeline weinrib ikat pillows at lost and found

17 > bespoke jeans at the stronghold 1895

18 > feal mor balaclava and sweater at union

19 > le maroc pour elle perfume by andy tauer at scent bar

20 > natalia brilli leather coin purse at bon & ging

where to lay your weary head

there's many great places to stay in los angeles, but here's a couple of my picks:

edgecliffe house
silver lake
323.661.5440
www.houseinsilverlake.com
weekly rate: $1100.00
notes: pretend your a local, and rent this one-bedroom home in the hills

villa delle stelle
6087 harold way - hollywood
323.876.8100
www.villadellestelle.com
suites: $180 - $285 daily, $1080 - $1260 weekly
notes: glam, yet affordable suites in hollywood

vibe hotel
5920 hollywood boulevard - hollywood
866.751.8600
www.vibehotel.com
premium private: $75 - $62 daily traveler dorms: $19 - $22 (!!) daily
notes: cheap and chic motel, right in the action of hollywood

venice suites
417 ocean front walk - venice
888.829.7417
www.venicesuites.com
suites: $90 - $180
notes: affordable suites by the beach

others:

the standard (hollywood & downtown): www.standardhotel.com
kor hotels (viceroy, maison 140, avalon hotel, chamberlain): www.korhotelgroup.com
sofitel los angeles (west hollywood): www.sofitella.com
élan hotel modern (west hollywood): www.elanhotel.com

los angeles

note: all maps face north

neighborhood overview

note: all maps face north

malibu / topanga / santa monica / brentwood

eat

e03 > axe
e04 > baby blues bar-b-q
e05 > beechwood
e19 > empanada's place
e20 > ford's filling station
e34 > stroh's gourmet
e38 > 3 square bakery/
rockenwagner bakery

shop

s13 > firefly
s27 > pamela barish
s30 > patio culture
s45> the stronghold 1895
s46> tortoise

note: all maps face north

venice / mar vista / culver city

eat

shop

note: all maps face north

fairfax district / mid-city / hollywood

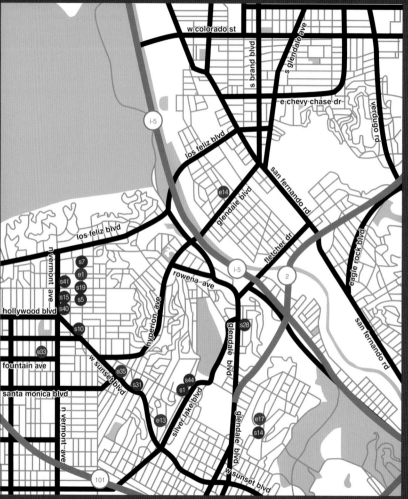

note: all maps face north

los feliz / atwater village / silver lake / echo park / eagle rock

note: all maps face north

boyle heights / chinatown / downtown

alcove cafe & bakery

a cafe and bakery

1929 hillhurst avenue. betweeen clarissa and franklin avenues
323.644.0100 www.alcovecafe.com
mon - wed 6a - 11p thu - sat 6a - midnight sun 7a - 11p

opened in 2004. owner: tom trellis
$ - $$: visa. mc
breakfast. lunch. dinner. brunch. coffee/tea. treats. beer/wine
first come, first served

los feliz > **e01**

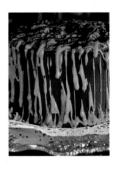

welcome to *alcove cafe's* land of plenty. plenty of pastries, cakes, tarts, salads and sandwiches. loyal fans come here knowing they'll get plenty of big, you-won't-go-hungry portions. i cross my heart; the omelettes come from ostrich eggs! there's cozy seating inside if you're sun resistant, but for those who crave al fresco dining, aim outside for one of la's primo dining patios. every day at the *alcove* feels like sunday brunch, and that's a plenty good feeling.

imbibe / devour:
alcove's secret recipe sangria
brioche french toast
alcove burger
crab cake sandwich
filet mignon wrapped in bacon on crispy greens
americano layer cake
pineapple upside-down cake
almond tart with seasonal fruit

auntie em's kitchen

cozy country-style restaurant and fine food market

4616 eagle rock boulevard. corner of corliss street
323.255.0800 www.auntieemskitchen.com
restaurant: mon - fri. 8a - 7p sat - sun 8a - 4p
marketplace: mon - thu 9a - 8p fri 9a - 9p sat - sun 9a - 7p

opened in 2002. owner/chef: terri wahl
$ - $$: all major credit cards accepted
breakfast. lunch. dinner. brunch. coffee/tea. treats. catering
first come, first served

entering *auntie em's kitchen* is everything you want it to be, with a dash of kitsch. terri serves up tasty, satisfying meals and decadent desserts in her cheerful café. one minute the sweet aroma of baked goods wafts by. the next minute you sniff something savory and intoxicating. ding dong, your hunger is dead. don't forget to stop by the marketplace next door, where a great array of gourmet foods allows you to take a bit *auntie em's* goodness home. you don't even have to click your heels three times.

imbibe / devour:
homemade raspberry lemonade
mint ice tea
cowgirl creamery organic mt. tam cheese
jasper hill farms everything
chicken pot pie
green chili & white bean chicken chili
brownies with walnuts
farmers' market dinner nights

15

axe

vibrant, eclectic california cuisine
1009 abbot kinney boulevard. between brooks avenue and broadway
310.664.9787 www.axerestaurant.com
lunch tue - fri 11:30a - 3p brunch sat - sun 9a - 3p
dinner tue - thu 6 - 10p fri - sat 6 - 10:30p sun 5:30 - 9:30p

opened in 1999. owner/chef: joanna moore
$$: all major credit cards accepted
lunch. dinner. brunch. reservations recommended

venice >

i'm a slight bit jealous of my friend debra who lives in venice near *axe*, a restaurant for which we share intense love feelings. she makes a point to eat at *axe* at least once a week, but if she had her way, she'd move in. i imagine there are many people who have this fantasy, but how would the rest of us get a table? fear not—no camp cots are allowed. instead you'll find farm-fresh seasonal produce transformed into vibrant, uncomplicated food, seasoned simply to amplify its natural flavors. perfection.

imbibe / devour:
keenum breakfast tea
ozeki karatamba sake
poached eggs with stewed greens & bacon
crispy polenta with wild mushrooms
seared sake marinated fillet of beef
trout with cabbage, lentils & spinach
half roasted free-range chicken
homemade cardamom ice cream

baby blues bar-b-q

hybrid bbq and soul food

444 lincoln boulevard. corner of sunset avenue
310.396.7675 www.babybluesbarbq.com
mon - thu 11:30a - 10p fri - sat 11:30a - 11p sun noon - 10p

opened in 2004
owner/chefs: danny fischer and rick mccarthy grill master: eddy hernandez
$ - $$: all major credit cards accepted
lunch. dinner. reservations accepted for parties of six or more

venice >

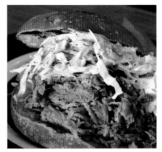

my godson sage and i discovered this spot while he was skating the venice boardwalk a couple of years ago. since that fateful day, we couldn't wait to return. we've explored bbq in many zip codes in this city, but we've found that *baby blues* satisfies above all the others. why? it's a mix of bbq grooves: north carolina meets memphis meets kansas city by way of ireland. the meats are all done to perfection and so finger-licking good that i could drink their bbq sauce. one visit and you'll get those bright baby blues.

imbibe / devour:
fresh brewed sweet tea
virgil's micro brewed ginger ale
baby back rack
memphis style ribs
carolina pulled pork
beer braised beef brisket
black jack's shrimp po' boy
peach betty

beechwood

modern dine and drink bistro

822 washington boulevard. corner of abbot kinney boulevard
310.448.8884 www.beechwoodrestaurant.com
sun - mon 6 - 11p tue - thu, sat 6p - 1a fri 5p - 1a

opened in 2004. owners: nick roberts, brooke williamson, david and patty reiss
chef: brooke williamson
$$: all major credit cards accepted
dinner. full bar. private parties. reservations recommended

venice > **e05**

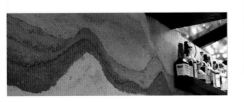

the combination of refined architecture and sharply executed interior design can really give one a rapturous feeling. you'll feel this at *beechwood* with its beautifully designed expanse of wood slats, low sectionals and warm glow lighting. though entranced by the chic surroundings, you'll be equally in love with the cuisine, which is comfort food elevated. the gang at *beechwood* have created the ultimate grown-up, hip playground—but please, no squabbling and take note, sharing will get you a gold star.

imbibe / devour:
prickly pear marguerita with sugar rim
spa-water martini
spanish onion soup
roasted spaghetti squash gratin
amusing ground rib eye burger
braised boneless shortrib
meyer lemon bars with
    warm blueberry compote & ginger gelato

21

beverly hills juice

seasonal and organic pressed juices
8382 beverly boulevard. between north orlando avenue and kings road
323.655.8300 www.beverlyhillsjuice.com
mon - fri 7a - 6p sat 10a - 6p

opened in 1979. owners: david and jennifer otto
$ - $$: cash
breakfast. lunch. first come, first served

west hollywood > **e06**

long before i moved to los angeles, my friend stephen would rave about a juice place in his neighborhood where he would start his day with the fresh-pressed apple triple ginger juice. immediately after i moved to town, i put *beverly hills juice* on my go-to list. at *b.h.j.* only the ripest, in-season, organic fruits and veggies go into the press and then the fresh, fresh, fresh juices are poured into eco-bottles made from corn. good for them, good for me and good for all.

imbibe / devour:
e3 live
pear double ginger juice
watermelon juice
apple mint coconut juice
almond banana manna (ice cream alternative)
strawberry apple banana manna shake
gerta's cookies
sergio's enchiladas & tacos

bld

modern american cuisine

7450 beverly boulevard. corner of north vista street
323.930.9744 www.bldrestaurant.com
daily 8a - midnight

opened in 2006. owners: amy knoll fraser and neal fraser chef: neal fraser
chef de cuisine: mike garber
$$: all major credit cards accepted
breakfast. lunch. dinner. brunch. full bar
reservations accepted for parties of six or more

mid-city > e07

though referred to often as a café, *bld* is so much more. brought to us by the team from nearby grace, *bld* takes the concept of the neighborhood café and elevates it. my favorite feature here is the 'have it your way' aspect to the menu. i'm the sort who could skip eggs first thing in the morning but instead would love nothing more than having a choice of charcuterie and artisanal cheese. no problem. want a porkburger instead of a hamburger? will do. see how this works?

imbibe / devour:
lavender dry soda
stone 'the arrogant bastard' ale
housemade pastries & muffins
ricotta blueberry pancakes
charcuterie & artisan cheeses
self-constructive dinner
berkshire porkburger
housemade ice cream

bluebird café

a sunny café
8572 national boulevard. corner of hayden avenue
310.841.0939 www.bluebirdcafela.com
mon - fri 8a - 4p

opened in 2005. owners: vincent treviño and chris marble
$ - $$: all major credit cards accepted
breakfast. lunch. brunch. treats. coffee/tea. beer/wine
first come, first served

culver city >  **e08**

in the heart of industrial culver city sits *bluebird*, a sun-drenched café you'd expect to find nestled somewhere in the countryside. vince and chris have created an oasis here of community spirit fueled by excellent food. the presence of this café gives this warehouse wonderland known as culver city a warm neighborhood vibe. from out of the industrial void comes everyone from worker bees to parents with hungry, wild-eyed kids just out of school. they all know that this is the place to come for a bit of calm and good eats.

imbibe / devour:
mint iced tea
breakfast panini
meatloaf with caramelized onions & gruyère
aged cheddar cheeseburger on brioche
chicken melt
iceberg wedge with blue cheese & onions
prix fixe backyard bbq in summer
coconut cupcake

bob's coffee and donuts

fresh-baked donuts, treats and coffee
6333 west third street. between fairfax and south ogden
323.938.1919
mon - sat 6a - 9p sun 6a - 8p

opened in 1927. owner: bob tusquellas
$: cash
treats. coffee/tea. first come, first served

fairfax district > **e09**

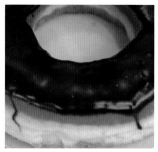

lots of practice went into perfecting the donut at *bob's*. i swear, they are the perfect confection: light as a feather and not too sweet. for generations both locals and visitors alike have made a beeline to this corner of the farmer's market, undeterred by the other food vendors tempting them. i suggest parking at the east end of the market, so you can go straight to the source. and what to order? classic is best—the airy raised glazed paired with the miraculously delicious coffee is the cure for anything that ails you.

imbibe / devour:
mexican custapec coffee
pasquini espresso
donuts:
  raised glazed
  cake
  chocolate caramel nut
jelly bismark
apple fritter

boule

haute modern french chocolatier and pâtisserie
420 north la cienega boulevard. between rosewood and oakwood avenues
310.289.9977 www.boulela.com
mon - sat 10a - 7p sun noon - 6p

opened in 2004. owners: david and michelle myers pastry chef: michael brock
$$ - $$$: all major credit cards accepted
treats. coffee/tea. first come, first served

west hollywood > e10

boule is the pompidou center of all things chocolate (as opposed to the more staid louvre). this is a modern take on the haute french pâtisserie, where artisanal confections are presented in an airy, gallery like space. you can find the classics here like a perfect tarte tartin, but i suggest being bold and trying michelle's chocolates that feature daring taste pairings like rose with caramel—she's a master at creating sublime flavor sensations. the sensation you will feel is pure happiness.

imbibe / devour:
boule blend coffee
palais du thé
chocolate cannelais
the *boule* cake
osburo (lapsoung souchong) chocolate
baumanier (cardamom coffee) chocolate
tarte tatin
honey thyme ice cream

cafe mimosa

cozy french cafe with antiques and gifts
395 south topanga canyon boulevard. corner of fernwood pacific drive
310.455.4341
mon - sat 6:30a - 2p sun 7:30a - 2p

opened in 1994. owners: claire and larry cohn
$: mc. visa
breakfast. lunch. treats. coffee/tea. first come, first served

topanga canyon > e11

up in rural topanga canyon it seems like every last body starts the day at *cafe mimosa*. could it be claire's gentle, sunny disposition that draws folks in? the fresh-baked pastries? or is it the lovely french country antiques and plenty of cozy places to read the paper or catch up with a neighbor? it's no doubt, all of the above. sit inside in the dappled sunlight or out on the shady patio. either way, you could easily stay from croissant to quiche before realizing how many relaxed hours have gone by.

imbibe | devour:
ginger lemon tea
chai tea
roast turkey on french baguette
roast turkey grilled steak & onion sandwich
mamoud's scones
vegan chili
poached salmon salad
coming soon *the canyon bistro*

cafe nagomi

gourmet natural japanese cooking mobile kitchen
roving truck—check website, location changes daily
310.923.8515 www.cafenagomi.com
11a - 2:30p check website for days

opened in 2005. owner/chef: taka kuroda
$ - $$: all major credit cards accepted
lunch. catering. first come, first served

roaming > **e12**

it's common to see lunch trucks outside office buildings around town. since i'm not a big fan of artery clogging lardfests on wheels, i veer away from these mobile restaurants. until i discovered *cafe nagomi*. i know everything happens when it's supposed to, but this idea came just in the nick of time. six days a week taka parks his truck at various locations where he brings to the hungry masses organic gourmet japanese food. using only quality ingredients and healthy, traditional japanese recipes, every entrée is plate-licking good and even better, good for you!

imbibe / devour:
barley tea
green tea soy latte
seafood nagomi plate
kinoko salad
seafood poke
tofu karaage
brown rice balls with smoked black cod

cafe tropical

revered silverlake institution

silverlake: 2900 sunset boulevard. corner of parkman avenue
inside hollywood billards: 5750 hollywood boulevard. corner of wilton
323.661.8391
daily 6a - 10p

opened in 1974. owner: jeff bay
$: mc. visa
breakfast. lunch. brunch. treats. coffee/tea. first come, first served

silverlake / hollywood

for thirty-plus years *cafe tropical* has served many generations of silverlake denizens, and still today its appeal to all who've passed through its doors remains unwavering. colorful, bohemian and casual, there are no airs put on here (refreshing in this town)—just killer café con leche, cuban pressed sandwiches and excellent pastries. people (myself included) have been known to drive crosstown for the guava pastries only to be seduced into staying by the low key warmth. even if you're visiting from topeka, you'll soon feel like a local at *cafe tropical*.

imbibe / devour:
café con leche
fresh juices & frozen fruit shakes
guava pastries
classic cuban-pressed sandwiches
turkey bacon croissant
quesadilla (the light yellow cake kind)
almond cigars
quiche & salad

37

canele

mediterranean influenced bistro

3219 glendale boulevard. between brunswick and edenhurst avenues
323.666.7133
tue - sun 5:30p - 10:30p

opened in 2006. owners: jane choi and corina weibel chef: corina weibel
$$: all major credit cards accepted
dinner. first come, first served

atwater village > **e14**

in european restaurants it's not uncommon to share at a table and dine family style. at *canele* you have that option too. with the warm glow of candlelight and a nice glass of wine to break the ice, sitting around a table here with strangers feels more like a homey dinner party where everyone knows jane and corina, but not yet each other. and let me tell you, there's nothing like roast pork loin over polenta to forge new friends. whether at the communal table or at table for two, it's hard to miss the *mmms* and *ahhhs* peppered throughout the soft din of conversation.

imbibe / devour:
a donkey and a goat 3/13 wine
drappier brut natur champagne
celery root with capers, garlic & sherry vinaigrette
flageolets bean soup
pan-seared snapper with rice & shell beans
seared beef tenderloin with pommes anna
roast pork loin with soft polenta & greens
chocolate almond cake with vanilla ice cream

chameau

modern french moroccan restaurant
339 north fairfax avenue. between bevelry boulevard and oakwood avenue
323.951.0039 www.chameaurestaurant.com
tue - sat 6a - 11p

opened in 2004. owner: kelly klemovich   co-owner/chef: adel chager
$$: all major credit cards accepted
dinner. beer / wine. private parties. reservations recommended

fairfax district >  **e15**

eating at *chameau* is a vibrant experience. it's the coupling of the french and morrocan cuisines, and the prismatic décor that stimulates the sight, taste and smell senses. the restaurant is awash in jewel-toned light, and with the sparkle of the iridescent tile, you'll feel like you're in a treasure den. and adel builds upon this kaleidoscope with his vivid, yet delicately spiced morroccan specialties. it's a magic carpet ride at *chameau*, one that you won't want to end.

imbibe / devour:
pomegranate/ginger prosecco cocktail
moroccan mint tea
duck bastilla with sweet almonds & cilantro
housemade merguez sausages & couscous
vegetarian tasting platter
pan-fried herb-stuffed sardines
  with olive purée
bastilla au lait with wild berry creme & berries

41

colorado wine company

2114 colorado boulevard. between casper and north maywood avenues
323.478.1985 www.cowineco.com
tue - sat 11a - 9p sun 11a - 5p

opened in 2005. owners: john and jennifer nugent
$ - $$: all major credit cards accepted
online shopping. wine tastings and events. gift registries. gift baskets
first come, first served

eagle rock > **e16**

when you think about it, wine is nothing more than a bottled and fermented, grape juice soap opera. there are lots of plot twists in its lineage. this grape and that grape from village x begat that wine. new grapes come to town and shake everything up. like dynasty or the bible—everyone loves a good saga. john and jennifer at *colorado wine company* will gladly tell the tales of each bottle and then they will offer you a taste of the results. and you can do this while relaxing comfortably in the styling lounge, not huddled standing sheepishly in a corner. winos rejoice!

imbibe / devour:
fiddlehead cellars sauvignon blanc
sea smoke pinot noir
fabulous barolo's
meibo midnight moon sake
odysseus grenache
orin swift's "the prisoner" red wine
artisanal cheeses from auntie em's

delilah bakery

come in bitter, leave sweet!

1665 echo park boulevard. corner of lucretia avenue
213.975.9400 www.delilahbakery.com
wed - fri 6:30a - 3p sat - sun 8a - 5p

opened in 2007. owner: genevieve ostrander
$ - $$: all major credit cards accepted
lunch. treats. coffee/tea. local delivery. first come, first served

in contrast to all these elimination diets—the "no this, can't have that" type fast, i heartily subscribe to the return of the "i'm not denying myself anything" diet of wholesome goodness. hallelujah. in the time before pesticides and preservatives (the real offenders) people didn't fear a balanced three course meal. if you have a hard time remembering this, it will come back to you when you step into *delilah bakery*. it's pure sunnybrook farm here. sure there's butter and sugar—these are southern recipes after all. embrace moderation and you can embrace everything!

imbibe / devour:
individually brewed coffee
hot chocolate with marshmallows
lemon ricotta muffin
chocolate cupcake with jack daniels frosting
pecan bourbon pie
old-fashioned apple pie
roast beef sandwich on french bread
sausage & spinach quiche

dominick's

the classic los angeles italian-style steakhouse
8715 beverly boulevard. between san vincente and robertson boulevards
310.652.2335 www.dominicksrestaurant.com
sun - thu 6p - midnight fri - sat 6p - 1a

opened in 1948. owner: warner ebbink owner/chef: brandon boudet
$$: all major credit cards accepted
dinner. full bar. late night. reservations recommended

west hollywood > e18

dominick's opened not long after the last world war ended. today's restaurants feel lucky to make it through the first year—so staying open for 59 years is quite a feat. you'll find everybody here from the loyal regulars who could tell you the meals they ate in the '70s, to the newcomers who come in for the classic italian steakhouse menu. there's a feel of clubbiness at *dominick's*; though the velvet rope, studio 54 feeling is not what i speak of. more of the "i eat here once a week and know all the waiters' names," home-away-from-home feeling. classic.

imbibe / devour:
meyer lemon mojito
dominick's own "dago red" wine
fresh lump crab with shaved fennel
burratta & bresaola
rice balls with mushrooms & mozzarella
three-course sunday family supper
chocolate panna cotta with caramel sauce
affogato (vanilla gelato drowned in espresso)

empanada's place

argentinian food
3811 sawtelle boulevard. corner of venice boulevard
310.391.0888
tue - sat noon - 7p

opened in 1985. owner/chef: norma gill
$: cash
lunch. dinner. treats. coffee/tea. first come, first served

culver city > **e19**

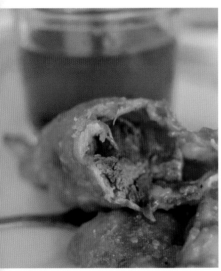

many countries, especially in south america and the caribbean, have a meal wrapped in pastry. none is as revered as the argentinian empanada. sound right up your alley? then head to the l.a. temple of this beloved food item, *empanada's place*. this is the perfect savory tide-me-over snack, when a late afternoon sweet treat might just put you over the edge. need more than a snack? order several different ones with a side salad and call it a meal. and for the ultimate argentinean experience, get the trifecta: mate, empanadas, and dulce leche.

imbibe / devour:
yerba mate (south american herb tea)
empanadas:
  arabe
  spicy beef
  papa con luesa
  pascunlina
  alfafore
dulce leche

ford's filling station

american regional cuisine

9531 culver boulevard. between cardiff and watseka avenues
310.202.1470 www.fordsfillingstation.net
mon - fri 11a - 11p sat 5 - 11p

opened in 2006. owner/chef: benjamin ford
$ - $$: all major credit cards accepted
lunch. dinner.   full bar. reservations recommended

culver city > **e20**

"making your way in the world today takes everything you've got. taking a break from all your worries, sure would help a lot. wouldn't you like to get away? sometimes you want to go where everybody knows your name." oh. excuse me, yes, i'll have a bacon cheeseburger. sorry, some places just take me there, *cheers* soundtrack and all. *ford's* is the essence of what makes a great neighborhood restaurant—a place where you really do leave your "whatever" at the door and dig into some supremely satisfying comfort food. i say, cheers to that!

imbibe / devour:
ford's filling station draft ale
flatbreads
brook trout
pub burger
kobe beef cheeks
crispy flattened chicken
seared diver scallops
butterscotch pudding

inaka

japanese natural food restaurant
131 south la brea avenue. between west first and second streets
323.936.9353
lunch tue - fri noon - 2:30p dinner tue - fri 6 - 9:45p sat 5:30 - 9:45p sun 5:30 - 9p

opened in 1979. owner: yuzuru j. abe
$$: all major credit cards accepted
lunch. dinner. first come, first served

inaka is one of my longtime favorite restaurants. i head here when my stomach is begging for some simplicity. it's for this reason, i recommend *inaka* for the traveler. after you've been eating high on the hog, multiple thanksgiving-style meals daily, trying more combinations of rich foods than you'd ordinarily have in a year, you want to eat no more—but you need your strength to carry on exploring. no worries, the macrobiotic, traditional japanese home-cooking here will balance you right out and you'll be back on the road again.

imbibe / devour:
virtual buddha gan bel tonic
ume sho bancha tea
red trout with kale, lotus root, hijiki & brown rice
kabocha pumpkin soup
japanese-style hot pots
inaka salad
seafood yosenabe
chocolate tofu mousse (my favorite!)

izayoi

inventive japanese cuisine and sushi
132 south central avenue. between east first and second streets
213.613.9554
lunch mon - fri 11:30a - 2p dinner mon - sat 5:30 - 10:30p

opened in 2005. owner/chef: junichi shiode
$$: all major credit cards accepted
lunch. dinner. full bar. reservations recommended

little tokyo > e22

artistically presented, gorgeous food can peak your curiosity and seduce you away from the comfort zone of your familiar cuisine. basically, the food looks so pretty you have to try it—for many americans that is how their love of sushi began. junichi, one of l.a.'s master sushi chefs further tempts the palate with his new restaurant, *izayoi*. enjoy the freshest of sashimi here, but take note—the real stars are the izakaya — beautiful tapas-size savories. my tip: start with the familiar favorites, but quickly branch out from there, as your love affair will undoubtedly grow and grow.

imbibe / devour:
sake
lotus root salad
cucumber with rice vinegar & seaweed
pork sirloin marinated in soukyu miso
steamed mixed mushrooms in ponzu
grilled sardines
seared beef sashimi
green tea ice cream with mochi & bean paste

la serenata de garibaldi

original east los angeles outpost for mexican dining
1842 east first street. corner of bailey street (see website for other locations)
323.265.2887 www.laserenataonline.com
sun - thu 11a - 10p fri - sat 11a - 11p

opened in 1985. owners: jose and aurora rodriguez chef: jose rodriguez
$$ - $$$: all major credit cards accepted
breakfast. lunch. dinner. reservations recommended

obsessed with the pulp fiction of raymond chandler? if you want a slice of the real deal, 21st century style, have lunch at *la serenata de garibaldi* in boyle heights. this is a neighborhood where generations have lived since it was still mexico—yet it's also close to l.a.'s fashion, judicial, financial and municipal centers. in this hacienda restaurant, the worlds converge: boxers meet with their lawyers, police captains lunch with d.a.'s, reporters interview sources, all of them savoring the classic mexican food covered with one (or two or three) of jose's famous salsas.

imbibe / devour:
sangria
over thirty salsas!
camarones gigantes en cilantro
salmon enchilada in chipotle sauce
mexican sea bass in cuitlacoche sauce
milanesa con papas
coconut flan
guava cheese cake

57

little next door

mediterranean artisanal market and café
8142 west third street. between south la jolla avenue and kilkea drive
323.951.1010 www.thelittledoor.com
daily 10a - 6p

opened in 2006. owners: frederic and nicolas meschin chef: t. nicolas peter
$ - $$: all major credit cards accepted
breakfast. lunch. brunch. treats. coffee/tea. beer/wine. grocery
first come, first served

aix en third street is what i've decided to rename this neck of the woods. one step onto the tiled terrace of *little next door* and you've left this city far behind. here you'll find an artisanal market the likes of which you'd expect to find in provence. this is not just any old french deli, but a bit like a mini *fauchon* with its authenticity, quality and sublime gastronomy. but of course it's perfect, as this is the sibling to *the little door*, a restaurant which is verging on legend status. the food is so spot-on here that even a bite of the jambon beurre on baguette is like a trip to france.

imbibe / devour:
ripassa by the glass
côte de brouilly
jambon de paris avec buerre &
  cornichon on baguette
salmon en croûte
bittersweet valrhona flourless chocolate cake
organic farm-fresh housemade pickles & jams
little door signature harissa

59

lou

intimate and cozy eating house

724 north vine street. between melrose and camerford avenues
323.962.6369 www.louonvine.com
mon - sat 6p - midnight

opened in 2006. owner: lou amdur
$$: all major credit cards accepted
dinner. wine. monday night suppers
reservations accepted for parties of six or more

hollywood > **e25**

when i found out that l.a. architect and tastemaker barbara bestor consulted on the design of a restaurant in the heart of hollywood, i made a beeline to its door. i was not disappointed. *lou* satisfies on so many levels: first, the thrill of adventure—the place is virtually invisible as it's camouflaged within a nondescript strip mall. second, the cozy décor and staff—the marimekko prints are as friendly as the informative staff who knowledgeably guide you thru the smart and interesting wine list. third, the slow food menu and pig candy—don't ask, just go try.

imbibe / devour:
old world riesling tasting
monkey & son espresso
pig candy!!!
armandino batali salumi
house-smoked duck & hook's ten-year-old
    cheddar crostini
oyster nights
valrhona pot au chocolat

61

magnolia

classic american cuisine

6266 1/2 west sunset boulevard. between vine street and argyle avenue
323.467.0660 www.magnoliahollywood.com
daily 11 - 2a

opened in 2005. owners: laurie mulstay and ron marino
$$: all major credit cards accepted
lunch. dinner. brunch. full bar. late night. reservations recommended

magnolia is the unstuffy, yet refined restaurant that heralds the rebirth of hollywood proper. laurie and ron serve american classics here with above par attention to flavor— nowhere is this more evident then the vegetable plate. huh? that's right, it's a revelation in simplicity. as i shot this entrée its fragrant aroma took over and i found myself furtively nibbling away, turning the plate, then coming in closer with the camera to hide the missing vegtables that were happily in my stomach. and the best part is that you can eat this well until the kitchen closes at 1am. brilliant!

imbibe / devour:
ginger cosmo
magnolia gimlet
awesome organic vegetable plate
tuna tartare, avocado salsa & tobiko caviar
lobster ravioli
seared ahi tuna
new york strip steak
mint chocolate chip ice cream sandwich

malibu seafood

excellent fresh fish market and patio café
25653 pacific coast highway. between malibu and corral canyon roads
310.456.3430 www.malibuseafood.com
daily 11a - random, seasonal, sunset-ish closing

opened in 1972. owners: wayne caywood, john christensen and mark ridgway
chef: michelle ridgway
$ - $$: mc. visa
lunch. dinner. byob. first come, first served

my friend jamie first took me here during one of my early visits to los angeles. now, any trip up p.c.h. must include a swing thru *malibu seafood*—it's like a culinary toll i gladly pay. the love fest started with fish 'n' chips, then malibu locals tressa and kazi alerted me to the wonders of the ahi burger and chowder—lord, i've been converted. eating fresh seafood while sitting on a warm, breezy perch over-looking the sparkling pacific ocean is the stuff of fond, tear-producing memories. i suggest you try it for an ultimate los angeles experience.

imbibe / devour:
cola with lemon
ahi tuna burger
squid steak sandwich
fish & chips
steamed mussels or clams in garlic broth
clam chowder in a bread bowl
grilled pacific red snapper with rice pilaf &
    coleslaw

65

mao's kitchen

super-fresh, country style chinese cooking
venice: 1512 pacific avenue. corner of zephyr court. 310.581.8305
mid-city: 7315 melrose avenue. between fuller and poinsettia. 323.932.9681
www.maoskitchen.com
sun - thu 11:30a - 10:30p fri - sat 11:30 - 3a

opened in 2007. owner: jake li
$ - $$: all major credit cards accepted
lunch. dinner. byob. delivery. first come, first served

venice / mid-city > **e28**

the widespread use of preservatives and additives have given chinese food a bad rep over the years. jake at *mao's kitchen* is doing his part to undo this perception. starting with his venice location, *mao's kitchen* quickly gained a reputation for fresh, healthy chinese food, a friendly staff and delicious recipes that use pure ingredients. *mao's* was a hit! imagine my glee when i happened upon the new location, only days old, while strolling around my neighborhood—healthy chinese within walking distance! jake, i thank you on behalf of my entire neighborhood.

imbibe / devour:
fresh homemade ginger ale
jasmine iced tea
orange-ginger chicken
long march camp-fry
peace not war wonton
model citizen noodle soup
shao mountain lamb
red bean pastries

milk

old school ice-cream palour and cafe
7290 beverly boulevard. corner of north poinsettia place
323.939.6455 www.themilkshop.com
sun - thu 9a - 10p fri - sat 9a - 11p

opened in 2007. owner/chef: bret thompson pastry chef: richard yoshimura
$ - $$: all major credit cards accepted
breakfast. lunch. dinner. brunch. treats. coffee/tea. first come, first served

mid-city > **e29**

anyone who really knows me, knows that i think milk, the liquid from cows, is a four-letter word. that is, unless, we are talking milk by-products, like ice cream. then, i have nothing but love. i have a favorite brand, flavor and memory for every city i have ever lived in or visited. when i was a kid in nyc, summers meant going for a cone after dinner with my family. later on in high school, summers were spent scooping. since i've lived in l.a., there's been no ice cream memories made—until now. *milk* is all that and more; in fact, it's now my favorite four-letter word.

imbibe | devour:
old-fashioned milk shakes, malts & floats
espresso à la mode
 oreo crunch ice cream bar
sandwiches:
  coffee crunch ice-cream
  inside-out grilled ham & cheese
  media noche pressed
milkies

69

moishe's / moishe's village

fine middle-eastern cuisine
6333 west third street. between south fairfax avenue and ogden drive
323.936.4998
daily 9a - 9p

opened in 1992. owner: movses aroyan
$: cash only
lunch. dinner. first come, first served

fairfax district > **e30**

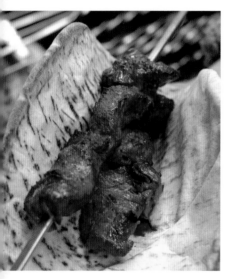

los angeles is a bustling multi-culti metropolis, so you've got to appreciate the mere existence of the farmers' market here. young and old and in-between; locals from differing sectors of the city and tourists from around the world flock to this historic food court. one of my favorite stops? *moishe's* stalls. i love the roasting and grilling meats that are seasoned and cooked to their caramelized, savory best; the salads that are tangy and crisp; and what can be said about the light-as-air falafel other than, hey, how'd they do that?

imbibe / devour:
pomegranate juice
awesome falafel
boerek (open-faced baked sandwich)
mouhamara (walnut & pepper dip)
chicken shawarma
kebobs!
bulgar pilaf
baklava

pacific dining car

beloved fine-dining steakhouse
downtown: 1310 west sixth street. corner of witmer street
santa monica: 2700 wilshire boulevard. corner of princeton street
213.483.6000 www.pacificdiningcar.com
open 24 hours daily!

opened in 1921. owner: wes idol III (fourth-generation owner) chef: berty siegels
$$ - $$$: all major credit cards accepted
breakfast. lunch. dinner. brunch. afternoon tea. full bar. late night
reservations recommended

downtown / santa monica >

for ben, the night owl in my life, two a.m. is just the right time for a full-course meal. if we are not at home slow-roasting some elaborate after-midnight meal, we're on the lookout for delicious late-night dining options. beyond greasy spoons or thai food, the pickings are pretty slim for fine dining past ten pm. we do have one place though that we go to over and over again—the legendary *pacific dining car* which is built like a series of old-fashioned dining cars, but roomier. here you can have your perfectly cooked, fine-aged steak and eat it too—at three a.m.!

imbibe / devour:
fresh orange juice
eggs blackstone
pancakes with pacific dining car sausage
the lobster appletini
cowboy steak
filet mignon with baked potato & the trimmings
apple tart tartin with apple calvados ice cream
pacific dining car steak relish

port royal

traditional jamaican cuisine

1412 broadway. corner of fourteenth street
310.458.4147
mon - sat 11a - 8p

opened in 2003. owner/chef: zoja reid
$ - $$: all major credit cards accepted
lunch. dinner. first come, first served

santa monica > **e32**

many santa monica residents in the know think of *port royal* as a great place to get authentic jamaican cuisine to-go. this is absolutely true as, yes, zoja's got her jamaican cuisine down pat—it's classic and truly tasty. but don't be in a rush to grab your food and go because eating here is half the experience. the combination of the colorful décor and the cool ocean breezes blowing in, make you feel transported to the islands. think of it as a mini-vacation without the kitschy island theme park vibe.

imbibe / devour:
dg old jamaican ginger beer
natural juices: pineapple ginger & sorrel
curry shrimp
jerk chicken
oxtail stew
beef patties
curry goat
coco bread

square one dining

natural is always best and nature is not a trend

4854 fountain avenue. bewtween north edgemont and berendo streets
323.661.1109 www.squareonedining.com
tue - sun 8a - 4p

opened in 2006. owner: phil fox chefs: robert lee and hayden ramsey
$ - $$: all major credit cards accepted
breakfast. lunch. brunch. coffee/tea. beer/wine
reservations accepted for parties of ten or more

i love the sound of *the beatles* in the morning. as a child, my days often began with "good day sunshine" while eating breakfast and then i'd head off to school with the rest of the album echoing in my head. imagine my nostalgia to hear those morning songs while breakfasting at *square one*. the folks here understand how to start the morning—not only with good music but also with simply beautiful food. so instead of dreading the day, head here to chill out, have a lazy breakfast and hum a couple of tunes—the day will seem brighter, i guarantee.

imbibe / devour:
fresh-squeezed oj
american coffee
brioche french toast
baked egg-braised mustard greens with
   mushrooms & shaved gruyere on grits
pressed ham sandwich
toast with housemade jellies
the deconstructed chocolate cake

stroh's gourmet

extra special neighborhood delicatessen
1239 abbot kinney boulevard. corner of santa clara avenue
310.450.5119
mon - sat 7a - 7p sun 8a - 6p

opened in 2003. owner / chef: jason stroh
$ - $$: all major credit cards accepted
breakfast. lunch. brunch. treats. coffee/tea. beer/ wine. first come, first served

venice > **e34**

stroh's is the ultimate corner deli. how do i love thee? let me count the ways. #1, it's casual and unpretentious here. #2, the sandwiches are exceptional and imaginative without trying too hard and the ingredients are superior. #3, jason supports local food purveyors. #4, jason loves the potato maybe more than me. his french fries are perfect, i tell you. and what's a sandwich without some chips? *stroh's* stocks a crazy variety—brands that i've never seen before. there's a chip for every mood and every season—it's truly a potato wonderland.

imbibe / devour:
bridgit's b chai
abbondio pompelmo & fragola soda
madhouse munchies
fantastically fantastic french fries
potato fingers
ham sandwich on pretzel bread
locally baked cookies & baked goods
dr. bob's handcrafted ice creams

the cheese store of silverlake

cheese, wine and fine foods store
3926 - 28 west sunset boulevard. corner of sandborn avenue
323.644.7511 www.cheesestoresl.com
mon 10a - 6p tue - sat 10a - 6:45p sun 11a - 5p

opened in 2003. owner: chris pollen
$$: all major credit cards accepted
grocery. first come, first served

silverlake > **e35**

i love discovering new cheeses and in a shady corner of the sunset junction complex, there beckons *the (inspiring) cheese store of silverlake*. there's a miss marples village feeling to this complex, but the store itself is anything but small town—the selections here are culled from around the world. chris offers a vast variety of cheeses and all the fine things that go with them like hard-to-find brands of crackers, wines and olive oils. want a little bread to go with your cheese? fresh loaves are delivered daily. you'll go in for one delicacy but leave happily with many, many more.

imbibe / devour:
robert foley claret
extra virgin cold pressed
  umbria & arbequina olive oils
neal's yard dairy gubbeen
brin d'amour sheeps milk cheese
tarentaise alpine raw milk organic cheese
mcquade's celtic chutneys
nomu spices

the hungry cat

seafood. rawbar. cocktails

1535 north vine street. between west sunset boulevard and selma avenue
323.462.2155 www.thehungrycat.com
lunch tue - fri 11:30a - 2:30p dinner mon - sat 5:30 - midnight
sun brunch 11a - 3p dinner 5 - 10p

opened in 2005. owners: david lentz and suzanne goin chef: david lentz
$$: all major credit cards accepted
lunch. dinner. brunch. full bar. reservations recommended

the hungry cat sits curled up discreetly in a back corner of the sunset and vine complex. surrounded by hollywood's skyscrapers, it's a shady modern nook for this urban oyster shack. my pal jamie and i love to sit at the counter, front row center, feasting on the fruits of the sea, sipping fresh fruit or herb-infused cocktails, watching the theater of the kitchen unfold. we come again and again for the innovative but uncomplicated flavor combinations—pairings that awaken the senses and make the tastebuds beam, leaving nothing on the plate. no wonder the cat's hungry!

imbibe / devour:
cocktails:
  the elysian fields
  basil gimlet
oyster, clams, peel & eat shrimp
dungeness crab with blood oranges & frisee
roasted barramundi with celeriac puree &
  wild mushrooms
chocolate bread pudding

the oinkster

a fast-food restaurant with a slow-food vibe

2005 colorado boulevard. corner of shearin avenue
323.255.6465 www.oinkster.com
mon - thu 11a - 10p fri - sat 11a - 11p sun 11a - 9p

opened in 2006. owner/chef: andre guerrero
$: all major credit cards accepted
breakfast. lunch. dinner. treats. first come, first served

eagle rock > e37

PB&JELL
CUPCAKS

it's the year of the pig! and right on time, big as the day is long, stands *the oinkster*. pull over and check out this glorified, revamped, roadside dining experience. this is how fast food should be: high-quality food that takes time to create, but then served up lickety-split. andre is filipino and he infuses aspects of his culture (and its love of the pig) in this classic americana menu. natch, the pulled pork is off the hook and you must try the ube shake (it tastes coconut-ish)—it's destined to be a cult classic.

imbibe / devour:
oinkster orangeade & lemonade
ube shake made with fossilman's
  taro root ice cream & ube purée
pulled-pork sandwich
cheese burger
house-cured pastrami sandwich
valrhona hot fudge sundae
peanut-butter cupcake

3 square bakery + cafe / röckenwagner bakery

german & austrian inspired bakeries

3 square: 1121 abbot kinney boulevard. between westminster and san juan. 310.399.6504

r bakery: 12835 washington boulevard. between beethoven and moore. 310.578.8171

www.3squarecafeandbakery.com / www.rockenwagnerbakery.com

3 square: mon - fri 7a - 6p sat - sun 9a - 4p

r bakery: mon - fri 7a - 2p sat - sun 8a - 2:30p

opened in 2007. owner: hans rockenwagner chef: wolfgang gussmach

$ - $$: all major credit cards accepted (cash only at röckenwagner bakery)

breakfast. lunch. treats. coffee/tea. first come, first served

these related bakeries are sooo great, that featuring just one would just not do. there's *3 square bakery and cafe* in venice, which is the newer and larger of the two. then there's *röckenwagner bakery* in mar vista where wolfgang bakes, with precision, all of the german-inspired delights. wednesday and friday may bring a cavalcade of berliner fienders, but i am obsessed with the pretzel and the steiner breads. again, who could choose between the two? i can't, so thank you, i'll take both.

imbibe / devour:
julius meinl coffee
swiss bina peach ice tea
ed & pete's old-fashioned lemonade
berliners on wednesdays, fridays & sundays!
brie, caramelized pears & figs on walnut bread
bacon & cheese pretzel twists
bavarian meatloaf on pretzel bread
steiner (whole grain bread)

via cafe

vietnamese cafe and art house
451 gin ling way #8. bewtween north broadway and hill street
213.617.1481
sun, mon, wed 10:30a - 8:30p thu - sat 10:30a - 11p closed tuesday

opened in 2004. owner: amanda phan   chef: diane xui
$: all major credit cards accepted
lunch. dinner. first come, first served

chinatown >

in the heart of old chinatown is a sun-filled cafe and art gallery called *via cafe*. all day the tables turn with a steady stream of folk from nearby galleries, artist studios, fashion showrooms and tourists exploring the sites. it's an eclectic mix, but they all come here for diane's perfectly priced, freshly prepared vietnamese food. i come here for the chargrilled beef over noodles, but sometimes i change and have the shrimp noodle soup, though i do love the crackling spring rolls... ok, so i love the entire menu!

imbibe / devour:
blended green iced tea with boba
spring rolls
shrimp rice noodle soup
roast cornish game hen
grilled lemongrass steak over noodles
crispy sole with watercress vinaigrette
shaking beef

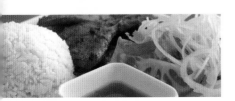

vincenti

modern italian classics

11930 san vicente boulevard. bewteen montana avenue and south bundy drive
310.207.0127 www.vincentiristorante.com
lunch. fri. noon - 2p. dinner. mon - sat. 6 - 10p

opened in 1997. owners: maureen vincenti and nicola mastronardi
chef: nicola mastronardi
$$$: all major credit cards accepted
lunch. dinner. full bar. reservations recommended

brentwood > e40

vincenti's could easily be the best italian restaurant in in town. descendant of the famed *rex*, its provenance is impeccable. today, chef nicola just slays us (us meaning all of los angeles) with his modern regional italian cuisine. simply put, he has the touch… and the flavor, texture, taste combinations and presentation. you want to cheer *bravo!* or weep with gleeful satisfaction after every bite. and then, there's maureen who makes you feel like a long-lost friend within minutes of meeting. exceptional food, warm greetings… *vincenti's* is worth all the stars in the galaxy.

imbibe / devour:
gaja conteisa (nebbiolo langhe) 1996
prix fixe menu regionale
housemade gnocchi with lobster,
  fresh cherry tomatoes, basil
wild boar sausage with braised cabbage
monday night pizza
affogato
grappa

notes

eat

shop

a + r

well edited global design store
1716 silver lake boulevard. corner of effie street
323.913.9558 www.aplusrstore.com
tue - fri noon - 7p sat - sun 11a - 7p

opened in 2005. owners: andy griffith and rose apodaca
all major credit cards accepted
online shopping

silver lake > s01

my friends jim and fidelma live in new england where they endure a seemingly endless winter. when i visit them during the freezing months, we spend a lot of time hanging around their cozy house where the days' activities include serial cat-napping and the roasting of select meats. so when i spotted the felt slippers at *a+r*, i knew i would be buying some of these to gift on my next northern visit. i can see us now, shuffling around in a food-induced stupor, clutching sections of the *new york times*, circling the couch for a nap landing, toes all toasty and warm.

covet:
malin collection knotted & beaded jewelry
scanwood pestle & mortar
sarah finn laser-cut wood coasters
maxim velcovsky porcelain vase
pia wallen felt slippers
keisuke saka paper model robots
gold bank in the form of a pig

95

apartment number 9

casual, yet polished clothing for men
225 twenty-sixth street (brentwood country mart)
between san vincente boulevard and la mesa way
310.394.9440
mon - sat 10a - 6p sun 11a - 6p

opened in 2004. owners: amy and sarah blessing
all major credit cards accepted

santa monica > **s02**

attention male shoppers: you are now entering an emporium of the chic, casual, timeless—where there are comfortable essentials for every man's wardrobe. there are no formal suits at *apartment number 9*, but in this industry town, who needs them as casual is the new professional. from fine cottons to cashmere, the sisters blessing have sourced far and wide to put a little oomph and spark into the usually staid world of shirts, t's, pants and shoes. this current, yet classic selection is perfect for men who claim to hate shopping (you know who you are).

covet:
seize sur vingt shirts
inhabit cashmere
james perse short sleeved brushed cotton polos
rogan everything
nsf sweaters & t's
cashmere & angora knit hats
band of outsiders everything
steven alan suede sneakers

black sheep knittery

quality knitting boutique featuring specialty yarns
6324 yucca street. between vine and ivar streets
323.464.2253 www.blacksheepknittery.com
mon - wed, fri 11a - 6p thu 11a - 8p

opened in 2004. owner: kristal moffett
all major credit cards accepted
online shopping. gift registry/wish list. classes. consultation

hollywood > s03

ama, my seven-year-old goddaughter, has taken up knitting. this confirms it: yucca street between vine and ivar might as well be fifth avenue in nyc during the easter parade—there's something for everyone on this little stretch of street. in keeping with the block's unspoken dictum of quality, rarity, and vibrant color, *black sheep knittery* aims to please, inspiring everyone to take up knitting. seeing the skeins, touching the yarns, you'll want to sit around the table and make a cozy scarf, hat or sweater right there on the spot.

covet:
yarns:
   woodstock handspun wool
   la lana native plant-dyed handspun wool
   fleece artist (nova scotia)
   manos del uruguay women's collective in a
   multitude of hues
great books & patterns
knitting accessories

blends/06+

sneaker boutique / high-end cult designer boutique for men and women
125 west fourth street. between south spring and main streets
213.626.6607 www.blendsus.com
mon - sat 11a - 7p sun 11a - 6p

opened in 2006. owner: tak kato and mike toe
all major credit cards accepted

downtown > **s04**

knowing that *blends* was located downtown, i came expecting a spare, modern boutique. and i was right. but nothing prepared me for the mother lode hidden within. up front, this place is all about the rare sneaker freaker business, but then you find yourself walking down a corridor, and a door slides open and on the other side is a sort of kafka/beckett-esque fashion jail. look behind the bars here at *06+* and you'll find supremely wearable offerings from some of my fave and soon-to-be fave world-class, avant-garde designers. pinch me.

covet:
sneakers:
  25th anniversary nike air jordans
  visvim
  marc jacobs sneakers
martin margiela everything
raf simons everything
hussein chalayan everything
hazel brown patchwork shearling jacket

bon & ging

real girl's clothing and boutique
1755 hillhurst avenue. corner of kingswell avenue
323.664.6688 www.bonandging.com
fri - sat noon - 6p sun noon - 4p and by appointment

opened in 2006. owners: grace and nanette sulland
all major credit cards accepted
online shopping. custom orders

los feliz > **s05**

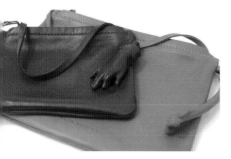

contrary to tabloid coverage, not every girl in l.a. is an aspiring actress devoted to tank tops, short shorts, flip-flops, and a ginormous 'it' bag. here there is also a tribe whose members work in the galleries, the museums or the studios, and they want to dress in expertly cut clothes that you won't see on everybody who walks down the street (yes, people walk in l.a.). whether it be a chic coat dress or a sweet blouse— these ladies know to shop at *bon & ging* where grace and nanette's big-city clothes hit the spot.

covet:
bon & ging:
  raw silk hemp coat dress
  silk jacquard shift dress with open back
  gorgeous skirts & blouses
bless soccer purse
momo suzuki leather bowls
natalia brilli leather coin purse
gwen frostic printed cards

103

calleen cordero

fine handcrafted leather footwear, clothing and accessories
7384 beverly boulevard. between north martel and fuller avenues
323.934.5541 www.calleencordero.com
mon - sat 10a - 6p

opened in 2005. owner: calleen cordero
all major credit cards accepted
online shopping

mid-city >

growing up in nyc, a walking city, i have always had an appreciation for the cobbler. every neighborhood in my city had one back then. it was probably then that my lifelong love affair with handcrafted leather shoes and accessories began. *calleen cordero* shares this love and takes it to the next level with her gorgeous, supple, hand-crafted leather pieces. calleen's designs are simple yet are utterly unique. once you own a pair of her shoes, you'll keep them for a lifetime, and the streets of the world will thank you.

covet:
india two wedge
kahlo wedge
twyla slipper
frida sandal
selma bag
lei belt
agate guitar strap
fiora corset

carol young undesigned

eco-chic clothing

1953 1/2 hillhurst avenue. corner of clarissa avenue
323.663.0088 www.carolyoung.com
tue - sat noon - 6p sun noon - 5p mon by appointment

opened in 2006. owner: carol young
all major credit cards accepted
online shopping. custom orders. 1% for the planet member

los feliz > s07

sometimes while researching these books you find yourself drawn to the same thing subconsciously. you find a store you like, see something, then realize you've seen it before. that was my one degree of separation with carol at *undesigned*. i shot a picture of her skirt at *satya* in philly, kaie shot (and bought) a dress at *impulse* in seattle and now here i was with her laughing at the small-worldness of it all. there's a reason people from coast to coast love *undesigned*— it's clothing that's well-cut and flattering to every physique. every closet needs a piece (or more)!

covet:
undesigned:
  pleated micro fiber travel ware
  peekaboo shrug
  koala crop hoodie
  bamboo denim ciao skinny jeans
moon alley handcrafted candles
whitney smith pottery
yeh laser-cut leather handbugs & wrist cuffs

107

claire joseph

ready-to-wear and couture clothing
6322 yucca street. between vine street and ivar avenue
323.461.7911 www.clairejoseph.com
tue - sat. 11a - 6p mon by appointment

opened in 2000. owner: claire joseph
all major credit cards accepted
custom orders

hollywood > **s08**

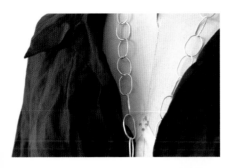

i don't know anyone who loves fine textiles more than claire. maybe more than color and pattern, i get the feeling it's the weight, drape and texture of the fabrics that inspire her the most. when you visit *claire joseph*, you'll see bolts upon bolts of vintage european fabrics, the likes and quality of which are unmatched by modern material. claire then creates from this treasure trove of materials (both vintage and modern) simple, exquisite clothing that ranges from wedding dresses to circle skirts to bags, each piece more beautiful than the next.

covet:
dresses:
  pleated cocktail
  slip
  bias
  custom wedding
sheer plaid shawl
collared blouse
mobius scarf

des kohan

modern and sophisticated feminine boutique

671 cloverdale avenue. between wilshire boulevard and west sixth street
323.857.0200 www.deskohan.com
mon - wed 11a - 6p thu 11a - 7p fri - sat 11a - 6p

opened in 2005. owner: desiree kohan
all major credit cards accepted
online shopping. custom orders. personal styling. private shopping

hollywood > s09

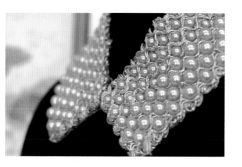

forget "what would jesus do?" instead ask yourself: "where would holly golightly go… shopping?" i know the answer. today's audrey hepburn would shop at *des kohan*. the 21st century holly still wants uncomplicated but structural, chic clothing. something feminine but not frilly for cocktails and whatever else her social calender demands. she'll blithely mix new designers' pieces with her vintage givenchy accessories. here you'll find all that you need for day, night, day into night… heck, i'll have a cocktail while envisioning the new holly's whirlwind life.

covet:
des kohan dresses & belts
giulia piersanti knits
vena cava everything
viktor & rolf shorts
ritsuko shirahama puff sleeve jacket
catherine holstein tunic dress
vintage gucci, hermès & givenchy accessories
annie costello brown accessories & jewelry

distant

turkish imports and home décor

4516 hollywood boulevard. corner of hillhurst avenue
323.669.0829 www.distant-la.com
tue - sat 11a - 7p sun noon - 5p

opened in 2006. owners: arzu and robert benavides
all major credit cards accepted
online shopping. gift baskets

los feliz > **s10**

my friend jamie zipped into *distant* one day on her way to a meeting, and since then found herself pining to return. for someone with an extraordinary business of her own (*lost and found*) to say that, to me, is the highest endorsement. so off i went. jamie speaks the truth. the store is full of carefully selected textiles, ceramics and chandeliers mostly from turkey. arzu has an impeccable eye for design and quality. we bonded instantly—the moment i left my new friend i wanted to do a full-blown update of my home: from bedding to turkish towels for the bath.

covet:
turkish 100% cotton towels & robes
bedding, cushions & pillows
hand-blown glass & wrought-iron chandeliers
leather purses in every color, please!
vintage uzbeki suzanis
handmade felt & cowhide rugs
olive oil soaps
felt hats

113

dosa818

extraordinary nature and ethnic-inspired shopping experience
818 s broadway 12th floor. between west eighth and ninth streets
213.627.3672 www.dosainc.com
wed - fri by appointment

opened in 2003. owner: christina kim
all major credit cards accepted

downtown > s11

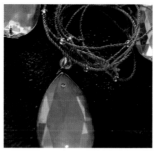

high above the hubbub of downtown is a heavenly cloud of inspiration and wearable, ethnic-inspired fashion. for close to twenty years christina kim has created gorgeous clothing, drawing influences from her world travels, the natural elements and art. the admiration for her and her clothing line, *dosa*, is now worldwide. i invite you to come to the unparalleled *dosa* experience. a soaring, light-filled penthouse loft, filled with magical vignettes. this is a one-of-a-kind shopping experience that feels like visiting a museum of wonder.

covet:
dosa:
  standard issue striped t's
  liberty of london print everything
  iridescent leather ottoman
  khadi silk wrap dress & slip
  jacob lawrence inspired collection
pippa small 24k gold jewelry
maasai collection beaded bracelet

family

exceptional store of books, printed matter, and other media
436 north fairfax avenue. between rosewood and oakwood avenues
323.782.9221 www.familylosangeles.com
daily 11a - 7p

opened in 2006. owners: david kramer and sammy harkham
mc. visa
online shopping. on-site artist studio upstairs

fairfax district > **s12**

turn off your computer. put down your cell phone. get out of the house. it's time to rediscover printed matter. you might not be looking for anything in particular, but you'll find the obscure, the amusing and the graphically appealing at *family*. it's all i can do to not froth on about all the books, music and design goodities they have here. trust me when i say, you probably haven't experienced this type of browsy wide-eyed wonder since you first learned to read, were set loose in a bookstore and told to get anything you liked.

covet:
what is the what by dave eggers
kramers ergot 6 edited by sammy harkham
great selection of local independent labels
jordan crane wallpaper & silkscreens
kinky friedman everything
mika miko
kurosawa's yojimbo
shoboshobo tree sweater

117

firefly

eclectic, ever-loving gift shop

1413 abbot kinney boulevard. between california and milwood avenues
310.450.6288 www.shopfirefly.com
mon - sat 11a - 7p sun 11a - 5p

opened in 1999. owner: erinn berkson
all major credit cards accepted
online shopping. gift registries. gift baskets. custom orders

venice > s13

when i think of fireflies, i think of mid-summer dusks sitting on a porch following the flickering glow on the lawn beyond. *firefly,* the store, has the cozy vibe of the home you might enter after you've been lulled by this crazy dance of light. once inside this place, it's as if an invisible firefly leads you around. your eyes dart and dance from one nook to another, room to room, alighting on all the treasures. this is a home you'll have a hard time leaving.

covet:
cake everything
edge recycled wood frames
bla bla baby knits & t's
robeez baby booties
bob's your uncle coral plates
julie rofman jewelry & art
pamela barsky goods
erinn's commitment to the local artists

flounce vintage

beautiful quality men's and women's vintage
1555 echo park avenue. corner of morton avenue
213.481.1975 www.flouncevintage.com
tue - sun 11:30a - 6:30p

opened in 2002. owner: lisa gerstein
mc. visa

echo park > 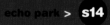 s14

one of the things i miss most about living in echo park is the ease with which i could frequent *flounce*. the inventory covers gloria swanson to jackie o, clark gable to james dean and everything in primo condition. i love visiting with lisa and whoever else happens to be in the store, merrily trying things on while chatting up a storm. when lisa says the experience at *flounce* is like shopping in auntie mame's living room—that about sums it up. bonus: this is real vintage, with a capital v, but not at sotheby's prices! now that's super swell!

covet:
`30s bias cut dresses
`40s rayon dresses
cashmere cardigan
assorted evening purses
bonwit teller hat box
men's `50s gabardine shirts
men's cuff links

gypsy's palace

a lush fabric salon

1730 north vermont avenue. bewteen kingswell and prospect avenues
323.662.5669 www.gypsyspalaceonline.com
mon - fri 10a - 6p sat 11a - 4p

opened in 2003. owners: jillian joy luellwitz, amanda marie and stacy ann finch
all major credit cards accepted
online shopping. custom orders. interior design consultation

los feliz > **s15**

rancho los feliz goes back to the 1700's. with grants from griffith's estate for the park and observatory, and the disney and sennett studios nearby—the area's residential development heyday came in the `20s and `30s. currently, los feliz is home to some famous sorts, but when i drive these streets i still imagine the stars of the silent era swishing around boudoirs in satin dressing gowns. the sisters of *gypsy's palace* see it too. they specialize in opulent fabrics, window treatments, and trimmings to make your home feel glamorous—the old guard would approve.

covet:
fabrics:
  hemp traders
  pindler & pindler inc.
  kravet design
  pucci-inspired silk prints
bedding
mokuba ribbon
tocca candles & lingerie

123

healing waters

136 north orlando avenue. corner of beverly avenue
323.651.4656
mon - sat 1 - 5p

opened in 1992. owner: jennifer otto
cash
acupuncture by appointment. gift registries. gift baskets. classes

west hollywood > s16

ever notice when you wear bright, vibrant colors, people respond to you positively? combine the power of color and pure essential oils, and the effect is extraordinary. at *healing waters* they draw upon this with their aura-soma color reading. it's a bit complex to explain in this tiny space, so you're best served to come here and experience how the choice of colors can reflect needs hidden deep within you. wow. in a crazy busy city like l.a., taking the time to keep your equilibrium in line is a good thing.

covet:
czech quartz nail files
aura-soma color readings
natural extracts of australia essential oils:
  ultimate eucalyptus
  tasmanian lavender
hawaiian fennel soap
green hope farms flower essences
baskets from kenya

125

hillary rush

chic and affordable clothing for women

8222 west third street. between south harper and la jolla avenues
323.852.0088 www.hillaryrush.com
mon - sat 11a - 7p sun noon - 5p

opened in 2005. owner: hillary rush
all major credit cards accepted
custom orders

west hollywood > s17

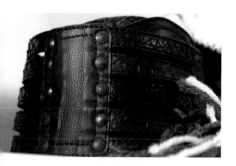

third-generation fashionista hillary is not distracted by the fickle trends of label lemmings. she knows what she and her customers like—classic, yet current styles at a range of price points. hillary specializes in rotational pieces, which is my new favorite fashion term as it best describes clothing that is of the moment style and proportion-wise, but not in a way that will make you cringe ten years from now. you wear the clothing now and feel fantastic, store it after the season is over, but when the season comes around again next year, the pieces will still feel fresh.

covet:
alexander wang
tysa everything
tree silk tunics
mimo clothing
jeffrey campbell's rush boot
super suite seventy seven shoes
j brand wide palazzo denim pants
manon von gerkan jewelry

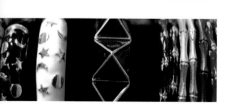

ige

eclectic asian-inspired lifestyle store
7382 beverly boulevard. between north martel and fuller avenues
323.939.2788 www.igedesign.com
mon - sat 11a - 6p

opened in 2003. owner: helene ige
all major credit cards accepted
custom orders

mid-city > **s18**

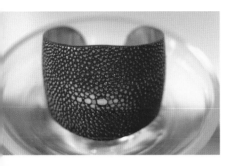

there are many artisans around the world making beautiful, useful objects that brighten our lives. there are also (thank goodness) a few discerning shop-keepers displaying and selling these crafts. at *ige* i'm reminded why i write these books: to inform and sometimes remind people (and that includes santa) about these special places. helene is that rare com-bination of both shopkeeper and artisan, so it feels doubly good to shout out to the world that *ige*, the store and the woman are exceptional.

covet:
ige birds of a feather mobile
artel etched glass bowl
steve vaubel aquamarine charm
wolfgang sirch bent plywood car & train
marilyn safran design 18k gold & citrine earrings
helene zubeldia red shagreen cuff
luc kieffer resin & swarovski crystal ring
hand-carved sandalwood bottles

keep

women's kicks (sneakers)

1757 hillhurst avenue. between melbourne and kingswell avenues
323.663.6900 www.keepcompany.com
wed - sat noon - 7p sun noon - 6p

opened in 2006. owners: una kim and margot jacobs
all major credit cards accepted
online shopping

los feliz > s19

it's no secret that we ladies have no problem suffering so we can sport some sexy heels. but finding sneakers that don't make you look like sporty spice or a starter for the l.a. sparks was next to impossible until *keep* came along. slip your tired hooves into a pair of their stylish kicks and it's like walking on a cloud—yes, support can be beautiful and stylish and eco-friendly and above all ridiculously comfortable. and warning: these sneakers aren't for performance unless dressing painlessly and stylishly is your sport.

covet:
kicks:
  nuss
  tobin
  benten
  duke
  guerra
keep close t's
owl sweatshirt

krislyn design

floral couture

6910 melrose avenue. between north sycamore avenue and orange drive
323.692.7862 www.krislyndesign.com
mon - fri 10a - 5p sat by appointment

opened in 2005. owners: krislyn komarov and nancy whitehurst
all major credit cards accepted
online shopping. gift registries. gift baskets. custom orders/design

hollywood > s20

have you ever thought you would be a good florist because you could create a pretty arrangement? think again. there's more to floral arrangements than bunching flowers and leaves together. what about bark? branches? crystals? mirrors? krislyn uses all kinds of organic matter to create magical compositions that more than brighten your day, they transport you. the atmospheric use of shapes, colors and textures offers a new appreciation of the elements. a trip to *krislyn design* is like a trip to narnia, a dream you never want to awake from.

covet:
krislyn's floral design anything
driftwood candelabra
hanging birch sleeve with air plants
succulent pods
portea
natenal gluska chainsaw furniture
madagascar sting ray candle

loft appeal

home décor
903 south hill street. corner of west ninth street
213.629.9105 www.loftappeal.com
daily 10a - 6p

opened in 2004. owners: rich reams and ron senger
mc. visa
custom orders

downtown > **s21**

already a must-stop for in the know prop stylists and production designers, *loft appeal* is also the decorating welcome wagon for the steady increase of people flocking to live downtown. developed in the early 20th century, downtown has been a financial, fashion and entertainment center throughout the years. now, it's having a renaissance as a residential area. moving into an open-plan loft but don't have a clue how to appoint the space? whatever your taste, the folks at *loft appeal* have something to help you realize your metropolitan dreams.

covet:
the juke box
chinese side table
lucite chair
ceramic lamp
faux fur throw
rattan arm chair
sarcasm society sign
vintage glass medicine bottles

135

lost & found stores

vibrant retail vortex

6314 - 6320 yucca street. between ivar avenue and north vine street

323.856.5872

mon - sat 10a - 6p

opened in 1999. owner: jamie rosenthal

mc. visa

hollywood >  s22

pretty much everywhere i go, i tell people about *lost and found*. so i know no one will be suprised when i say it's one of my favorite shopping destinations. in any city. period. infant to adult, clothing to books, furniture to toys—jamie's sense of color, pattern, texture, whimsy is the stuff i crave. more than just gorgeously designed product, *lost and found* is about community. when there was nothing on this quiet block, jamie created a vibrant retail vortex. pop in to any of the four storefronts and you're likely to run into a long-lost friend, or make a new one.

covet:
aris geldis paris jewelry
corita kent prints
lucky fish everything
k. jacques sandals
missoni towels sheets & throws
antik batik everything
madeline weinrib ikat pillows
allegra hicks clothing, gloves & bikinis

137

marcjoseph / kate

exceptional clothing and furnishings
7210 beverly boulevard. between north formosa avenue and alta vista boulevard
323.939.4600 www.marcjoseph.com
tue - sat noon - 7p and by appointment

opened in 2006. owners: marc joseph and kate cook
mc. visa
special events

mid-city > **s23**

once upon a time, marc and kate had their own separate stores. then one day they packed up their stores, and moved together to beverly—boulevard, that is. the old saying "two heads are better than one" comes to mind here because what they were doing seperately before is now a great mix of high end `50s to early `80s art, furniture and objets with designer vintage clothing. all is beautifully displayed to dramatic effect in this sweeping expanse. with the loot of these passionate collectors under one roof you can't help but strike it rich!

covet:
vintage clothing:
  missoni
  yves saint laurent
  omo norma kamali
  jean muir
karl springer dining table
dunbar furniture

marie mason

beauty product heaven

225 twenty sixth street (brentwood country mart). corner of san vicente boulevard
310.394.5710 www.mariemasonapothecary.com
mon - sat 10a - 6p sun 11a - 6p

opened in 2005. owners: marie mason and gary bushnell
all major credit cards accepted
gift registries. gift baskets. custom orders

santa monica > **s24**

as a toddler, my goddaughter ama had inconsolable tantrums. i would reach into my bag, pull out some delicious-smelling hand creme and begin to apply. her eyes would glaze over, crying would cease and with a sniffle she'd ask, "what's that?" storm cloud gone, crisis averted. oh, the soothing power of aromatic beauty products. in her sparkling bright salon of pampering, *marie mason* has some of the most luxuriously effective products in the free world! enter vexed, exit carefree. your radiant self will deflect any unpleasantries that cross your path.

covet:
santa maria novella
miller et bertaux
l'artisan parfumeur
napoleon perdis
100 % pure line
d.l. & co
kate somerville skin health experts
custom perfumes, oils & lotions

momo/shabon

vintage and recycled clothing and accessories
momo: 308 north stanley avenue. between beverly boulevard and oakwood avenue
shabon: 7617 1/2 w beverly boulevard between north stanley and curson avenues
momo: 323.964.5240 shabon: 323.692.0061 www.momopop.net
mon - sat noon - 8p sun noon - 6p

opened in 2000. momo owner: tetsuzo okubo shabon owner: rei fujii
all major credit cards accepted

mid-city > s25

were you ever friends with both a brother and a sister growing up? and when you'd drop by to visit, you'd end up wanting to spend time with both. *momo* and *shabon* are brother and sister stores. and like siblings, they are different, yet clearly related. *momo*, the brother store, carries recycled and vintage clothes for both men and women, up-and-coming japanese designers and lots of other collectibles. around the corner, *shabon*, the sister store is a pandora's box of girly vintage clothes and a staggering assortment of heels, bags and accessories. this is one stylish family!

covet:
vintage:
  levis & army surplus
  goyard luggage
alm cashmere jacket
john luke eastman art
vintage polaroid cameras
quilted ladies bolero jacket
saddle leather knee high boots

mrs. biederhof's

vintage and limited-edition contemporary eyewear
7911 rosewood avenue. corner of north fairfax avenue
323.782.0772 www.mrsbiederhofs.com
mon - sat 11a - 7p sun noon - 6p

opened in 2006. owners: sylvia bognar and javier brambila
all major credit cards accepted
online shopping. custom orders. licensed opticians.

fairfax district > s26

whether it be inside or outside, dark or light, day or night (i.e. the bright lights of the nighttime premiere), angelenos love, love, love their sunglasses. and the fictional *mrs. biederhof* feels one can never have too many of them—sun or reading or vision correction… you name it. you wear glasses daily, so why not change them often like you do your clothes, shoes and hopefully underwear. *mrs. biederhof's* stocks obscure brands and vintage and reissue frames that you won't find anywhere else. so go on then, make a spectacle of yourself.

covet:
françois pinton jackie & ari reissues
vintage ray-bans
vintage french deadstock
vintage dior, ysl, gucci & balenciaga
one-of-a-kind handmade frames
porsche carrera
cazal
persol

145

pamela barish

old-world couture and ready-to-wear

1327 1/2 abbot kinney boulevard. between cadiz court and andalusia avenue
310.314.4490 www.pamelabarish.com
thu - sat 11a - 5p mon - wed by appointment

opened in 2003. owner: pamela barish
all major credit cards accepted
custom orders/design

venice > s27

it's hard not to live or visit l.a. without thinking about what it must have been like back in its glamour hey-dey. i'm talking about the days of ava and cary and tyrone and rita—no last names needed. it's hard to find that old-school luxe today in the city of angels, but the essence of it is here at *pamela barish*. not only does pamela name her garments after some of these style icons, she understands the allure of be-witching clothing whether it be casual or premiere-ready. slip into a kate shirt-gown, and watch for all eyes to be on you.

covet:
kate double-layer silk charmeuse shirt gown
short kate in black eyelet with white slip
rita fitted sundress
ava short-sleeve fitted dress
jackie fan-sleeve coat
mary buck thompson crowns

147

panty raid

foxy lingerie

2378 1/2 glendale boulevard. corner of brier avenue
323.668.1888 www.pantyraidshop.com
mon - fri 11:30a - 7p sat noon - 7p sun noon - 6p

opened in 2002. owner: jen abercrombie
all major credit cards accepted
gift registries

silver lake > **s28**

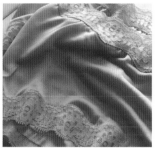

when it comes to my foundations, i like something more than the standard-issue basics and less than triple-x racy. the term for what i like is "fancy pants" and *panty raid* has a whole stash of them. they're colorful, pretty, comfortable and give coverage. yes, i said it, coverage. that's a feature i appreciate as i'm not one to expose my skivvies to the world. i believe it's called underwear because it's something you wear under your clothes. i also believe the same effort that goes into the outer should go into the under, and jen makes it easy to make the effort.

covet:
huit
mary greene
commando
elle macpherson intimates
eberjey
duets
only hearts
liz

149

particolare

jewelry and rare, exotic objects
6911 melrose avenue . between north sycamore avenue and orange drive
323.939.9098
tue - sat noon - 7p

opened in 2003. owner: ricardo and gina martin
all major credit cards accepted
gift registries. gift baskets. custom orders/design

hollywood > **s29**

at *particolare* there are many spectacular pieces on display from riccardo and gina's world travels. but if you want to indulge your inner contessa, come and see the exquisite jewelry. no disrespect, but aren't people a bit bored by the big-name jewelers? personally, i don't want the logo on the box to outshine me or the jewelry i'm sporting. if originality is your thing, ricardo is hollywood's secret weapon for jewels, with a capital j. you're precious, so why not wear something truly precious too?

covet:
ricardo martin fine fashion jewelry
vintage chinese snuff bottles
argentinian canes
chinese & indian vintage erotica
zanetto silver bowls
17th & 18th century spanish colonial
 santos sculptures
ann pamintuan wrought-iron furniture

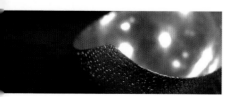

patio culture

outdoor living and entertaining store
1612 abbot kinney boulevard. corner of rialto avenue
310.314.9700 www.patioculture.com
tue - sat 11a - 7p sun noon - 5p

opened in 2006. owner: karla stevens
all major credit cards accepted
online shopping. classes in outdoor entertaining. custom orders

venice > **s30**

have you ever noticed the flikr ad on the apartment therapy site? the one with the lemon yellow lanterns and cushions? the ad you tag because you have to go wherever that photo was taken *tout de suite*? it was always a toss-up between go there and live there— whatever, because i saw myself there. then one fateful afternoon, while driving, i made a u-turn and literally parked right next to the aforementioned vignette and it was *patio culture*! the reality was even more glorious and colorful and all of the useful indoor/outdoor items became immediate must-haves!

covet:
patio culture citrus yellow with
  white trim cushions
lucite furniture
bauerkraft handcrafted tile & accessories
cloth:
  brunschwig et fils
  etamine of paris
  christopher farr

paulina quintana

modern & graphically-inspired children's clothing
1519 griffith park boulevard. corner of west sunset boulevard
323.662.4010 www.paulinaquintana.com
tue - fri 12:30 - 5p sat 9:30a - 5:30p sun 11:30a - 5:30p

opened in 2004. owners: paulina quintana and robert russell
all major credit cards accepted
gift registries. gift baskets

silverlake > s31

like marimekko, florence eisman, even lily pulitzer, *paulina quintana's* patterns and use of color are pleasingly, instantly recognizable. her playful but still sophisticated kids' clothes have us grownups begging, pleading and stamping our feet for something in our size too. paulina, please?! we've been good... it's just not fair! wait. i think she's heard our cries because with the advent of the bedding line, an adult's clothing line can't be far behind and then maybe, just maybe, our tantrums will subside!

155

persimmon

handpicked objects

310 north flores street. corner of beverly boulevard
323.951.9540 www.shoppersimmon.com
tues - sat noon - 6p and by appointment

opened in 2005. owner: julie schroeder
all major credit cards accepted
online shoping. gift registries. custom orders/design

west hollywood > **s32**

franco from *scent bar* told me about *persimmon* around the corner from his store. so i floated over on a magic carpet of fragrance to see what he was talking about. once inside i came down to earth quickly. rough cut, semi-precious gems will do that to a girl. it's jewelry galore here, displayed in natural dioramas and on rugged wood tables next to organic plant arrangements by *krislyn design*. and julie thoughtfully stocks horn bowls and exotic skin jewelry boxes to put your newfound treasures in. handpicked objects is an understatement; this is gift list central.

covet:
annette ferdinandsen gold sea fan earrings
jamie joseph green tourmaline ring
ninh wysocan gold dome earrings
priya himatsingka crochet rectangle ring
aurora lopez mejia gold imagination shield
r & y augousti exotic leather jewelry boxes
jeff benroth glass

planet maple skate & surf shop

supporting inner-city extreme sports

5011 west adams boulevard. bewteen south la brea and longwood avenues
323.734.2323 www.myspace.com/planetmaple
tue - fri 11a - 6p sat - sun noon - 6p

opened in 2006. owners: cedric bell and william lamar
cash only
classes. custom orders. indoor half-pipe

west adams > **s33**

far, not in miles but in lifestyle, from the vaguest hint of an ocean breeze, in the heart of l.a.'s concrete jungle, will and cedric opened a skate and surf shop called *planet maple*. here they share their love of board sports with youth who may not otherwise be exposed to it. why preach to the converted when you can share your passion and watch it flourish in the uninitiated? now there's a steady stream who sk8 the indoor halfpipe and meet on weekends for surf lessons. community fun, that's the *planet maple* way. if you build it they will come.

covet:
planet maple t's, hats & boards
sugar skateboard co.
organika skateboards & clothing
cali green beanies & sweats
freshjive caps
quicksilver everything
the kayo corp.

plastica

practical & fun housewares

8405 west third street. between south orlando and croft avenues
323.655.1051 www.plasticashop.com
mon - sat 11a - 6p sun noon - 5p

opened in 1996. owner: carla denker
all major credit cards accepted
online shopping. gift registries. gift baskets

west hollywood > s34

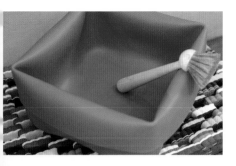

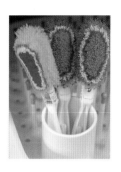

sim-sim-simma down now! times have changed and we're programmed to have a knee-jerk p.c. reaction to even hear the word plastic used. so let's consult the dictionary, shall we? plastic: capable of being shaped or formed. with this spirit of the law in mind, *plastica* is a temple of brightly colored, well-designed, practical, everyday items and toys for young and old. this is a place that celebrates—dare i say it? in swedish? form och funktion? i did. i had to. you need it. it looks good. it works. it's these qualities that make for giddy, guilt-free spending.

covet:
marimekko everything
bento boxes
green rubber wash-up bowl
lucky fish striped t's
`60s vintage plastic pillows
recycled celluloid prison rings
mighties magnets
egg bank

post26

stylish contemporary and vintage fashion emporium

225 twenty sixth street (brentwood country mart). corner of san vicente boulevard
310.451.0950
mon - sat 10a - 6p sun 11a - 5p

opened in 2006. owners: kay sides and jeannine braden
all major credit cards accepted
custom orders

santa monica > **s35**

some parties happen in the kitchen. some boil over in the basement, and some blow the roof off in the attic. *post26* would be the latter party variety. after warm greetings by the staff as you enter, you calmly make the rounds, taking in the choice collection of current brands beloved by all. after feigning calm, you then race upstairs to the attic loft, where you'll find a "celebrate good times, come on!" c-razy vintage designer heaven. those old-timers knew how to get down! new-timers rejoice!

covet:
clothing:
  alexander wang
  ports 1961
  maison simone
  lutz & patmos
  thread social
  nili lotan
aurora lopez mejia jewelry

push emporium

contemporary emporium

400 south main street. corner of west fourth street
213.617.1159 www.pushemporium.com
mon - fri 8a - 7p

opened in 2006. owner: sally daliege
all major credit cards accepted
dry cleaning. shoe repair

downtown > **s36**

anyone will tell you, doing errands in los angeles is a full-time job. so thank you sally, for taking the bore out of chores. at *push emporium* you've got the shopping covered with clothing by fresh local designers and also *dandelion ranch's* flowers, and then there's also a place to clean those new clothes: *dirty girl's dry cleaning* and whoeee, there's also shoe repair. at *push emporium* you can be au courant shopping for the latest fashions, and do your chores concurrently. that's some genius convenience!

covet:
so! skaars african print bags
12th street by cynthia vincent
private school saltwear
zuburbia vintage
mon petit oiseau
ag jeans
tuff gong
penguin

reserve

design and lifestyle store

420 north fairfax avenue. between oakwood and rosewood avenues
323.651.0131 www.reservela.net
tue - sat 11a - 7p sun noon - 6p

opened in 2006. owners: naama givoni and rick klotz
all major credit cards accepted
reserve radio. filmmaker spotlight

fairfax district > **s37**

all is not what it seems at *reserve*. yes, it's a brilliant design and lifestyle store where there's clothing; rare, out of print photo books and fresh design and pop culture tomes; a coupla turntables and a wall screen for movie screenings. but beyond the shopping experience, there's the feeling of being in a cool nightclub at *reserve* with its dark walls and conversation pit atmosphere. just block out the bright sunlight of the day outside, and immerse yourself in the mellow atmosphere that will entice you to hang out, take a load off and do a little conversing.

covet:
the age of adolescence by joseph sterling
  photographs from 1959-1964
graphis design 89
mike mills limited-edition ribbons
super rare serge gainsbourg dvd!!!
limited-edition reserve gear
banshee reserve & fresh jive t's collaboration
gonz!

167

scent bar

l.a.'s first fragrance boutique

8327 beverly boulevard. corner of north flores street
323.782.8300 www.luckyscent.com
tues - sat noon - 7p sun noon - 5p

opened in 2005. owners: adam eastwood and franco wright
all major credit cards accepted
online shopping. gift wrapping. custom orders.

west hollywood > **s38**

do you want to know what a specific small town in holland smells like? *scent bar* has a perfume that captures every grassy nuance. do you have memories of the intoxicating smell of tuberose and spices wafting in the evening breeze in morocco? save the airfare; there's a scent here that will take you there. franco and adam source the world over for exceptional, often exclusive, scents to suit men, women and the home. pull up a stool, share your deepest scent desires and within no time your every wish will be fulfilled.

covet:
le maroc pour elle by andy tauer
l'essence of mastenbroek
absolument absinthe
frankincense by regina harris
orange blossom room spray by jacques garcia
stoned by lynn harris
anat fritz eau de parfum for men

169

scout

forward fashion boutique
7920 west third street. corner of south edinburgh avenue
323.658.8684 www.scoutla.com
mon - sat 11a - 8p sun noon - 7p

opened in 2004. owners: greg armas and joey grana
all major credit cards accepted
online shopping

fairfax district > s39

a scout is someone who is sent ahead to look for new talent and discover things of interest. that's what *scout*, the store, is all about. greg and joey rigorously sift through both new and long-established designers and this yields unique pieces that fit into the forward-thinking aesthetic on display here. there was a vivienne westwood dress here that i lusted after—it could easily have been a bathrobe from the `40s, but felt at the same time singularly modern. genius. a bathrobe you can walk out of the house in with your head held high!

covet:
chamula cardigan
society for rational dress suede
  bucket bag & shoes
surface to air parka
clu tunic dresses
daughter of the sun jewelry
sonia rykiel navy bulky knit sweater
any overdyed black tunic

show

a modern lifestyle store

1722 north vermont avenue. between prospect and kingswell avenues
323.644.1960 www.showlifestyle.com
daily 11a - 7p

opened in 2001. owner: bradley cook
all major credit cards accepted
online shopping. gift registries. gift baskets. custom orders/design consultants

los feliz > s40

i know i use the word modern (a lot) in this book, and sometimes i branch out and use the word contemporary to mix things up. but what exactly does modern mean? these days an item can be modern if it's a reinterpretation of something vintage, or modern can be an item that's totally out there and super-futuristic. my suggestion is if you want to know what modern is, just visit *show*. it's the mix here that's modern. i can use a lot more adjectives, but i suggest you just pick yourself up and head to show for the visual story, as it says it all.

covet:
show revitalized vintage furniture
indoor / outdoor cut felt rugs
nama rococo & cavern wallpaper
l.e.d. stackable alarm clock
esque design reformed beer bottle vases
joseph albers in 1926 nesting tables
scrapile pressed wood benches

173

steinberg & sons/the little knittery

indie clothing boutique and knittery
4712 franklin avenue. corner of north vermont avenue
323.660.0294 www.steinbergandsons.com. www.thelittleknittery.com
mon - wed fri - sat 11a - 7p thu 11a - 9p sun 11a - 5p

opened in 1999. owner: suzie kim and julie edwards
all major credit cards accepted
gift baskets. classes. custom orders. free knitting patterns

los feliz > s41

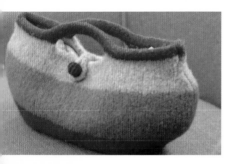

it's hard to believe now that just a couple of years ago, l.a. had only a teeny-tiny number of teeny-tiny boutiques that championed indy fashion designers. *steinberg & sons* was one of the leaders of the pack where many have since followed. men and women check in here regularly to get suzie's latest installment of limited soon-to-be classics while julie at the *little knittery* sources unique yarns for the knitting crew. as a result, their little shop is a coffee clatch of craftsmanship.

covet:
anzino & florence everything
envi jersey dresses
ronni kappos jewelry
augustine los angeles knit dresses
fremont men's corduroy parka
handspun one-of-a-kind yarns
cashmere reincarnation
joint venture knitting needles

sugar paper

print shop and more!

century city: 1749 ensley avenue. corner of santa monica boulevard
brentwood country mart: 225 twenty sixth street. corner of san vicente boulevard
cc: 310.277.7804 bcm: 310.451.7870 www.sugarpaper.com
mon - fri 10a - 6p sat 10a - 5p sun 11a - 5p

opened in 2003. owners: chelsea shukov and jamie grobecker
all major credit cards accepted
online shopping. custom orders/design

century city / santa monica > **s42**

i love my laptop and its conveniences as much as the next person, but my heart will always skip a beat for pen and paper. i carry more than one color signature pen, so you know my toes just splay when i hear the words letter and press put together. *sugar paper* has an assortment of gorgeous paper items—oh and the options! bring on the custom announcements and invitations, the greeting cards and the wrapping papers! polish your penmanship, friends, it's time to reclaim the mail from the likes of bill collectors.

covet:
sugar paper customs letter press
  stationary & invitations
cavallini circular paper clips
carrot & stick blank page notebooks
egg press cards
snow & graham cards & wrapping paper
lotta jansdotter baby wear
ribbons, ribbons, ribbons

surfas

restaurant supply and gourmet food paradise
8824 national boulevard. corner of washington boulevard
310.559.4770 www.surfasonline.com
mon - sat 9a - 6:30p sun 11a - 6:30p

opened in 1937. owners: les and diane surfas
all major credit cards accepted
online shopping. gift registries. classes / demos. custom commercial kitchens

culver city > s43

kitchen supplies and gourmet foods all in one place. no, you're not dreaming; at *surfas* you're in foodie heaven. even if you can barely boil water you'll be inspired to make something when you enter here. whether you have a restaurant kitchen to outfit or just need a toaster oven for your 250sq foot hollywood studio, *surfas* has something for everyone. but beware the dangers here. you may go in for just a whisk, but you'll leave with a bagful of goods. my weakness? the tea rose preserve so my toast won't be lonely.

covet:
surfas brand spices like black cardamom
lavender powder
trablit coffee extract
brittany fleur de sel
callebaut semisweet chocolate
sesame toaster
benriner mandolin slicer
loads of kitchen equipment

10 ten

modern furnishings
1724 1/2 silver lake boulevard. corner of effie street
323.663.3105
tue - sat 11a - 5p

opened in 1996. owners: scott and joanna nadeau
all major credit cards accepted
custom orders/design

silver lake > **s44**

in nyc, 1010 means news: "you give us twenty-two minutes, we'll give you the world." in silver lake, *10 ten* means clean-lined, modern art and furnishings. besides designing furniture that has achieved a cult following, scott has developed relationships with many an unsung design hero of the mid-century movement. as a native eastsider of l.a. where legendary modernist architects schindler and neutra built extensively, he'll gladly school you in the local lore, so give yourself at least twenty-two minutes here to absorb the beautiful designs and good conversation.

covet:
10 ten:
  upholstered couch
  table
ernesto gonzalez stripped bronze sculpture
eugene weston lll leather stool
david wilkens sculpture
architectural pottery & ceramics
stan bitters ceramics

the stronghold 1895

los angeles's original jean company
1625 abbot kinney boulevard. between venice boulevard and rialto avenue
310.399.7200 www.stronghold1895.com
mon - sat 11a - 7p sun noon - 6p

opened in 2006. owners: michael cassel and michael paradise
all major credit cards accepted
classes in denimology. custom orders

venice > **s45**

my friend j.p. who is an denimologist has guided me and our friend ben in our denim acquisitions for years. now we can return the favor. ben recently introduced me to the masterminds behind the resurrection of *the stronghold 1895*, a local denim line that dates back a century. here you'll find the finest in selvage denim, and you can buy off the rack or have a pair made to measure. you'll be in the hands of masters as ray (the manager) and the michaels have encyclopedic knowledge of all things denim and vintage americana, and they'll school you at the drop of an old stetson hat.

covet:
handmade premium denim jeans & jackets
antique watches & luggage
original carpet bags
filson tin coat
dominica bay rum
old pendleton blankets
white's boots

tortoise

all manner of mostly japanese objects

1208 abbot kinney boulevard. between san juan and santa clara avenues
310.314.8448 www.tortoiselife.com
wed - sun noon - 6p or by appointment

opened in 2003. owners: taku and keiko shinomoto
mc. visa
online shopping. gift registries. classes. custom orders

venice > **s46**

i am still abuzz from my visit last year to japan. the trip reinvigorated my appreciation for the japanese approach to space and nature—i experienced both in town (tokyo) and country (kamogawa). to feel this uniquely japanese approach and aesthetic stateside, visit *tortoise*. every object here sings the glory of the material it's made from, be it clay, paper, cast iron or wood—every element is exalted into useful, everyday items that beckon you to "touch me." i'll happily comply.

covet:
wappa bent cedar containers
sori yanagi elephant & butterfly stools
taku's furniture
1953 cast-iron paper weights
sori yanagi stained birch handle flatware
ubugi baby kimono
tenugui japanese traditional multi-purpose cloth
beautiful stationery & journals

turpan

stylish cleaning supplies and lifestyle boutique

225 twenty sixth street (brentwood country mart). corner of san vicente boulevard
310.451.9500   www.turpanonline.com
mon - sat 10a - 6p sun noon - 4p

opened in 2006. owners: greg and katherine turpan
all major credit cards accepted
gift registries. gift baskets. custom orders.

santa monica > **s47**

i'm not known for my cleaning skills, but i do love cool cleaning supplies and therefore i love *turpan*. if, like me, you are cleaning challenged, i suggest a lucite step stool to get you to the hard-to-reach places. feeling a bit more motivated? then greg will help you find all you need for the arranging and organizing of the beautiful things in your home, and he'll also stock you up with more beautiful things. makes me want to rush home and sweep, mop, dust, open all the windows and rearrange—no matter the season, it's never too soon for spring cleaning and shopping.

covet:
amazingly stylish cleaning supplies
julisis skin care
organic turkish cotton bath towels
bassamfellows stool
lutz & patmos cashmere throws
denis colomb scarves & blankets
c. hugo pott silver flatware

union

the godfather store of high-end streetwear
110 south la brea avenue between west first and second street
323.549.6950 www.unionlosangeles.com
mon - sat 11a - 7p sun noon - 6p

opened in 1994. owner: edward cruz
all major credit cards accepted

hollywood > **s48**

futurist engineer norman belle-geddes once said, "the highway must not intrude on the city, nor the city on the highway." so low-key, like it's hiding in plain sight, *union* is a clubhouse of quiet cool. i pass it almost every day and still had to be reminded where it was. eddie is the o.g., an original sponsor of this imaginary highway that links exclusive haute-urban streetwear and cult japanese and european brands with shops and collectors. that's why for fifteen years, with little fanfare, all roads on the streetwear fienders' map have lead here.

covet:
feal mor everything
random collectible collaborations
neighborhood
anything
visvim
maiden noir
wtaps
perks & mini

zenbunni gallery

organic high-quality arts and crafts

115 south topanga canyon boulevard, studio a. corner of old topanga canyon road
310.455.4351 www.zenbunni.com
by appointment or chance

opened in 2005. owners: zen and bunni wyldeflower
all major credit cards accepted
online shopping

topanga canyon > s49

as i approach topanga canyon, i always get this neil young soundtrack in my head, it goes something like "are you ready for the country?" mixed with "got to get away from this day-to-day running around." it's that last part that really speaks to this frazzled, city gal. ahhhh, topanga—breathe deep and smell the eucalyptus. it's rustic here, overgrown and mellow—an ideal place to woodshed. hence *zenbunni's*, a hothouse of creativity: her (bunni's) photos, his (zen's) sculptures, their t's and friends' products. it all makes for a lively convergence in this little utopia.

covet:
zenbunni organic t's, candles,
  clothes & jewelry
bunni's photography
zen's sculpture
melissa joy manning jewelry
lou zeldis vertebrae & seagrass bracelets
francisco mondet handmade luxury bags,
  accessories & furniture to order

notes

notes

previous edition businesses

**malibu / topanga /
santa monica / brentwood**

eat:

chez jay
manpuku
the counter
the arsenal

shop:

le sanctuaire
market
mini-market
weego home

venice

eat:

amuse cafe
jin patisserie
massimo's
wabi sabi

shop:

obsolete
salt

**fairfax district / mid-city /
hollywood**

eat:

angelini osteria
joan's on third
loteria grill
mashti malone's ice cream
musso & frank grill
off vine
pace
singapore's banana leaf
sona
table 8
the gumbo pot

shop:

c by karina
holiday
jack henry
kaviar & kind
ok
puppies & babies
room service
rosasen
silho
sonrisa
soolip bungalow
soolip papier and press
zelen

beverly hills / century city

eat:

clementine
graffeo
the cheese store

**los feliz/atwater village /
silver lake / echo park /
eagle rock**

eat:

alegria on sunset
blair's
casbah cafe
electric lotus
gingergrass
mexico city
silverlake wine
village gourmet

shop:

casbah cafe
le pink
patty faye
the kids are alright
yolk

*you can find the addresses
and phone numbers for all of
these businesses at our website: eatshopguides.com*

*if businesses that were fea-
tured in a previous edition are
not on this list, it means they
have closed.*

etc.

the eat.shop guides were created by kaie wellman and are published by cabazon books
for more information about the series: www.eatshopguides.com

eat.shop los angeles second edition was written, researched and photographed by agnes baddoo

editing: kaie wellman   copy editing: lynn king   fact checking: emily withrow
map design and production: play with numbers - jim anderson, erin cheek and kieran lynn

agnes thx: each and every businesses in this book. jp for first showing me the lay of the land. jamie for her friendship and for showing how to mix art, commerce and urban renewal. shamya and siddhartha for their charriot. kathi jo languid for her rallying pearls of wisdom. paul baddoo for his encouragement and support. ras benji, i'kl sage fiyah and ama terasu for being you.

cabazon books: eat.shop los angeles second edition
ISBN-13 978-0-9789588-0-0

every effort has been made to ensure the accuracy of the information in this book. however, certain details are subject to change. please remember when using the guides that hours alter seasonally and some-times sadly, businesses close. the publisher cannot accept responsibility for any consequences arising from the use of this book.

the eat.shop guides are distributed by independent publishers group: www.ipgbook.com

PRINTED IN SINGAPORE